I Wonder Why
The Sea
Is Salty

and other questions about the oceans

Anita Ganeri

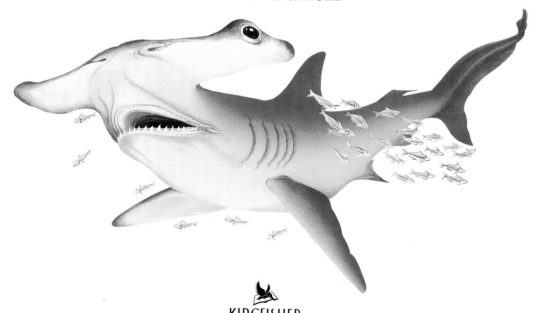

KINGFISHER
NEW YORK

Distributed in the U.S. by Macmillan, 175 Fifth Ave.,
New York, NY 10010
Distributed in Canada by H.B. Fenn and Company Ltd.,
34 Nixon Road, Bolton, Ontario L7E 1W2

Library of Congress Cataloging-in-Publication Data
Ganeri, Anita, 1961–.
    I wonder why the sea is salty/by Anita Ganeri.—
1st American ed.
        p.   cm.—(I wonder why)
    Includes index.
    1. Ocean—Juvenile literature. 2. Marine ecology
—Juvenile literature.   3. Marine Fauna   Juvenile
literature.
    [1.Ocean—Miscellanea. 2. Marine ecology—
Miscellanea. 3. Ecology—Miscellanea. 4. Marine
animals—Miscellanea. 5. Questions and answers.]
I. Title   II. Series: I wonder why
(New York, N. Y.)
GC621.5.G34   1995
551—46—dc20   94-30260 CIP AC

ISBN: 978-0-7534-5611-8

Kingfisher books are available for special promotions and
premiums. For details contact: Special Markets Department,
Macmillan, 175 Fifth Avenue, New York, NY 10010.

For more information, please visit www.kingfisherpublications.com

Printed in Taiwan
10 9 8
BTR/0609/SAP/RBM/126.6MA/F

Consultants: Michael Chinery, Keith Lye
Cover illustrations: Ruby Green, cartoons by Tony Kenyon
(B. L. Kearley)
Main illustrations: Chris Forsey 4–5, 6–7, 14–15, 20–21,
28–29, 30–31; Nick Harris (Virgil Pomfret Agency) 8–9;
Tony Kenyon (B. L. Kearley) all cartoons;
Nicki Palin 10–11, 18–19;
Maurice Pledger (Bernard Thornton)
16–17, 24–25; Bryan Poole
12–13, 22–23, 26–27

CONTENTS

How big is the ocean?

The ocean is truly ENORMOUS! It covers more than twice as much of the Earth as land does. In fact, it's made up of four oceans—the Pacific, the Atlantic, the Indian, and the Arctic. Although these all have different names, they flow into each other to make one huge world ocean.

● Don't go for a swim in the Arctic Ocean. It is the coldest ocean, and for most of the year it's covered in ice.

Which is the biggest ocean?

The Pacific is by far the biggest ocean in the world. It's larger than the other three oceans put together, and it's also much deeper. If you look at a globe, you'll see that the Pacific reaches halfway around the world.

What's the difference between a sea and an ocean?

People often use the words sea and ocean to mean the same thing. That's fine, but to a scientist, seas are just part of an ocean—the parts that are nearest to land. The Mediterranean Sea is between Africa and Europe, for example.

● These drops of water show the oceans in order of size.

Pacific
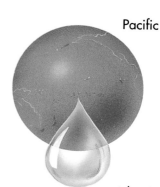

Atlantic

Indian

Arctic
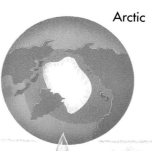

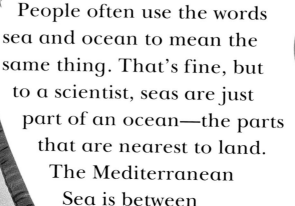

Why is the sea salty?

Seawater tastes salty because it has salt in it! The salt is the same as the stuff people sprinkle on food. Most of it comes from rocks on the land. Rain washes the salt into rivers, which carry it to the sea.

• Some of the sea salt we use comes from hot places, such as India. People build low walls to trap the seawater when the tide comes in. When the sun dries up the water, the salt is left behind.

• Most of the Earth's water is salty. Only a tiny part is fresh water that we can drink.

• Some beaches around the Black Sea are covered with rich, dark mud. People slap it all over themselves—it's supposed to be good for the skin.

Is the Red Sea really red?

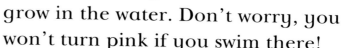

Parts of the Red Sea look red. In summer millions of tiny red plants called algae grow in the water. Don't worry, you won't turn pink if you swim there!

What did sailors fear the most?

In olden days, sailors had to put up with bad food, fearful storms ... and pirate attacks! Pirates roamed the high seas, on the lookout for merchant ships loaded with fine goods and treasure. When the pirates found a ship, they boarded it, attacked the crew, and carried off all the valuable goodies.

● Blackbeard was one of the most evil pirates. To look extra fierce, he used to thread rope through his beard and then set it on fire!

● Real pirates didn't actually make people walk the plank. But the pirates you read about in stories often do!

- There weren't many women pirates. Anne Bonny and Mary Read are two of the most famous. They disguised themselves as men.

Who first sailed around the world?

In 1519, a fleet of five ships set off from Spain to sail around the world. Their captain, Ferdinand Magellan, was killed on the way. Just one ship and 18 men completed the journey. It had taken three years.

- Times were tough for Magellan's men. When their food ran out, they had to eat cooked leather.

What is sand made of?

Look closely at a handful of sand, and you'll see that it's made of tiny chips of rock and seashell. The bits of rock come from cliffs that have been broken up by the rain and sea. The shells are washed in by the tide and crushed by the pounding waves.

● Not all sand is yellow. Some beaches have black, pinkish-white, or even green sand.

● Hang seaweed outside and it might forecast the weather! If it swells up, rain is on the way. If it dries out, then the Sun will shine.

● Wreckers were people who shone lights to trick ships into crashing on the rocks. Then they stole all the valuable things on board, and hid them in caves.

How are caves made?

As waves hurl sand and rocks against a cliff, it is slowly worn away. The waves scoop out a small hollow, then a deep hole. After a very long time, the hole is worn into a dark, damp, and dripping cave.

- A tropical beach may look deserted, but dozens of different plants and animals make their homes there.

- You can often find empty seashells washed up on the beach. Their owners have probably been eaten!

Why do limpets cling to rocks?

Like other animals on the seashore, limpets have a tough life. As the tide comes in, they are battered by the waves. As the tide goes out, they are tugged and pulled by the swirling water. The poor limpets have to cling tightly to the rocks so that they aren't swept out to sea!

Which fish has headlights?

Some fish make their own light at the bottom of the dark ocean. The anglerfish has a long fleshy "rod" dangling in front of its face. At the end of the rod is a blob that glows. Small fish are drawn toward the glowing light, only to disappear into the angler-fish's big, gaping mouth.

● The deep sea is inky black and as cold as a refrigerator. Even so, some amazing creatures live there.

Anglerfish

How deep is the ocean?

● The seabed has huge cracks in it, called trenches. Some are more than 6 miles deep.

Away from the shore, the ocean plunges to more than 2 miles in most places. That's deep enough to swallow 10 Empire State Buildings, one on top of the other!

Gulper eel

● Many deep-sea fish have really ugly faces. It's just as well it's dark down there!

What makes chimneys under the sea?

Fountains of boiling hot water gush out of holes in some parts of the seabed. Tiny grains sink down out of the hot water and build into weird-looking chimney stacks around the holes.

● Giant red-and-white worms as long as buses live around the chimneys.

Dragonfish

What's it like at the bottom of the sea?

You might think that the bottom of the sea is smooth and flat, but it isn't—at least not everywhere. There are mountains and valleys, hills and plains, just as there are on land.

- In 1963, a volcano erupted under the sea near Iceland. Hot, runny rock bubbled up to the surface of the water and hardened. It made a completely new island, which was named Surtsey.

- Along the shore, the land slopes gently into the sea. This slope is called the continental shelf.

- Flat plains cover half of the sea floor. They are called abyssal plains.

- The Mid-Atlantic Ridge is a long line of underwater mountains in the Atlantic Ocean.

Are there mountains under the sea?

Yes, lots—and they are all volcanoes! Someone has counted about 10,000 of them, but there may be double this number. The correct name for them is sea mounts. Some are so high that they stick out of the water and make islands.

● There are earthquakes under the sea, just as there are on land. In fact, there are over a million seaquakes a year! But most of them happen so deep down that we can't feel them.

● A trench is a deep valley in the seabed.

● A sea mount is an underwater volcano. There's a sea mount erupting somewhere as you read this!

How do fish breathe under water?

• Not all sea creatures can breathe under wat~~ Sea cows, seals, and dolphins breathe air, so they have to keep coming to the surface.

Fish have to breathe to stay alive, just as you do. But while you breathe oxygen from the air, fish take it from water. As they swim, fish gulp in water and push it out through slits called gills on their heads. Oxygen passes from the water into the fish's blood inside their gills.

Gill cover

How do fish swim?

Fish swim by using their muscles to ripple their bodies along. Wiggling their tails from side to side gives them extra push. They use their other fins to balance and change direction.

Which bird flies under water?

Penguins can't fly through the air because their wings are too short and stumpy. They are much more at home in the ocean, where they use their wings as flippers.

Which animal is jet-propelled?

● Seahorses aren't strong swimmers. They hang on to seaweed to avoid being swept away.

Squid don't have flippers or a tail, but they're still fast movers. They suck water into their bodies, then squirt it out so powerfully that their bodies shoot backward.

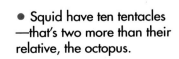

● Squid have ten tentacles —that's two more than their relative, the octopus.

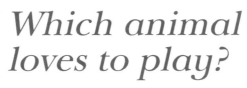

Which animal loves to play?

Dolphins are playful and trusting. Some are so friendly they will let you swim with them. Dolphins have even rescued drowning people, by using their noses to nudge them to shore.

How do whales and dolphins use sound to see?

Whales and dolphins use ears, not eyes, to find their way around. As they swim they make clicking noises, which travel through the water. When the clicks hit something solid, an echo bounces back—just like a ball bouncing off a wall. The echo tells the animal what lies ahead.

- Dolphins have up to 200 sharp, pointed teeth for holding on to slippery fish. Imagine brushing those every night!

- Narwhals are a kind of whale with a very long tusk. Sailors used to sell narwhal tusks, pretending they were the horns of unicorns!

Which sea animals sing like birds?

White beluga whales are nicknamed "sea canaries" because they cheep and chirp like birds. They can also moo like cows, chime like bells, or press their lips together with a loud smack!

What makes waves roll?

Waves are ripples of water blown across the surface of the ocean by the wind. On a calm day they hardly move, but in stormy weather they roll faster and faster, and grow higher and higher until they form huge walls of water.

● Make your own waves in a bowl of water. The harder you blow across the surface, the bigger the waves.

● Some waves are called white horses because their curly white tips look like horses' manes.

● At Waimea Bay, Hawaii, surfers ride waves up to 30 feet high—that's five times taller than a man!

- Palm trees will grow in a chilly place like Scotland because warm currents flow along the west coast, bringing water from much hotter parts of the world.

Are there rivers in the ocean?

The ocean has great bands of water called currents that flow like rivers. They travel faster than the water around them, moving from one part of the world to another.

- Ocean currents can carry a message in a bottle for you. But don't hold your breath. One floated for 73 years before it was washed up!

Why do sailors watch the tides?

Twice a day the sea comes high up the beach, and then goes back again. At high tide the water is deep, and sailboats can sail in and out of the harbor. But at low tide, the water is so shallow that sailors are either stuck on the shore or out at sea!

- In Canada's Bay of Fundy, the water at high tide is about 50 feet deeper than at low tide—that's the height of a five-story house!

Where do angels, clowns, and parrots live?

Angelfish, clown fish, and parrot fish are just some of the thousands of beautiful animals that live on coral reefs. Tropical fish like these often have dazzling colors and bold patterns.

Imperial angelfish

Parrot fish

● Coral reefs grow in shallow water in the warmest parts of the world.

Angelfish

● Giant clams live on coral reefs. Their shells are big enough to take a bath in!

What is a coral reef?

A coral reef is like a beautiful underwater hedge. It looks stony and dead—but it is really alive! Coral is made up of millions of tiny animals that leave their hard skeletons behind when they die. Each new layer piles on to the old, slowly building the coral rock.

● Corals come in all sorts of shapes—antlers, plates, mushrooms, feathers, daisies, and even brains!

Where is the biggest reef?

The world's biggest coral reef lies in warm shallow seas off the northeast coast of Australia. It's called the Great Barrier Reef, and it stretches for more than 1,200 miles. It's so huge that it can be seen by astronauts up in space.

Clown fish

Which is the biggest fish?

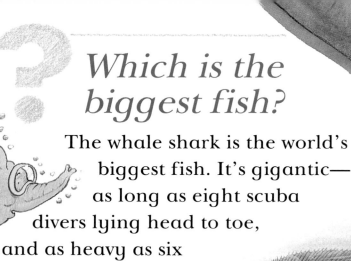

The whale shark is the world's biggest fish. It's gigantic—as long as eight scuba divers lying head to toe, and as heavy as six large elephants.

● The dwarf goby is the smallest fish in the ocean.

● The oar fish is the longest fish in the ocean—as long as four canoes placed end to end.

Oar fish

● The biggest sea plant is the giant kelp seaweed. A single strand can grow nearly as long as a soccer field!

Sailfish

Which is the fastest fish?

The sailfish can race along under water more than 60 miles an hour—as fast as a car. It tucks its fins in tightly, and its pointed nose cuts through the water like a knife.

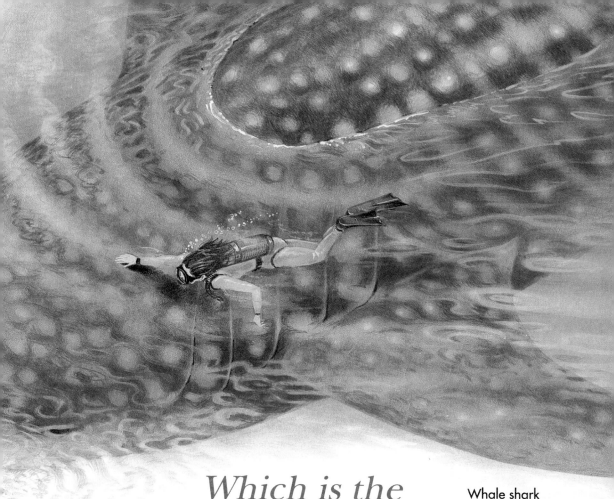

Whale shark

Which is the biggest crab?

● The pea-sized pea crab is the smallest crab of all. It lives inside oyster and mussel shells.

Japan's giant spider crab measures nearly 13 feet from the tip of one front claw to the tip of the other. It could open its arms wide enough to hug a hippopotamus!

Which fish hunts with a hammer?

The hammerhead shark has a huge head shaped like a hammer. But this tool is for hunting, not banging in nails. The shark's eyes and nostrils are at each end of the hammer. As the shark swims, it swings its head from side to side, searching for a meal.

● The Portuguese man-of-war catches its meal in its long, stinging tentacles.

Which is the most shocking fish?

Some fish give off electric shocks to protect themselves or to stun animals they want to eat. The most shocking ocean fish is the torpedo ray. If you could switch it on, it would light up a lightbulb!

● Thousands of mackerel swim together in one huge school. Their enemies find it difficult to pick out a single fish from the shimmering, silvery mass.

● The leafy sea dragon looks just like a ragged strand of seaweed. What a perfect disguise!

Which fish look like stones?

Stonefish look just like lumps of stone, or rock—but they're far more dangerous. If attacked, a stonefish uses the needle-sharp spines on its fins to stab its enemy with a deadly poison.

How deep do submarines dive?

Few submarines can dive much lower than 700 feet below the surface of the ocean. That's about 100 times deeper than an Olympic swimming pool.

What dives deepest?

Divers use smaller craft called submersibles to explore deep water and to look for wrecks and sunken treasure. The *Titanic* was an enormous ocean liner that sank over 80 years ago. Divers discovered the wreck 12,000 feet down in 1985. They were able to reach it in a submersible named *Alvin*.

● The *Titanic* was launched in 1912. On its very first voyage, it hit an iceberg and sank in the Atlantic Ocean.

Which was the deepest dive ever?

In 1960 two men dived nearly 7 miles into the Marianas Trench in the Pacific Ocean. They were inside one of the very first submersibles, an incredibly strong craft called *Trieste*. The submersible took about 5 hours to reach the bottom.

● Divers wear special suits of armor in deep water. This one is called *Spider*. It's like a one-person submarine!

● In the deepest parts of the ocean, the water would press down so hard that it would be like having ten elephants sitting on top of you!

Who fishes with fire?

On an island in the Pacific Ocean, people fish in the darkness of night. They set fire to the branches of coconut trees, and then hang them over the side of their boats. The fish swim toward the firelight —only to be caught by the islanders' sharp spears.

● Seaweed is rich in goodness, so farmers spread it on their land to improve the soil. It is also used to thicken icecream and toothpaste.

Are there farms under the sea?

Yes, but there aren't any farmers, cows, or sheep! Some kinds of fish and shellfish are raised in large cages out at sea. The fish are so well fed that they grow much more quickly than they would do in the wild.

• People all around the world have different legends that tell how the world was created. Some say that it was made inside a giant clam shell. It must have been some shell!

Are there jewels in the sea?

• The biggest pearl ever found was as large as your head. Imagine wearing that pearl around your neck!

In warm tropical water, pearls may grow inside the shells of oysters and clams. The pearls are such rare finds that they are very valuable. People risk their lives diving down for them.

Index

A
abyssal plain 14
Alvin 28
angelfish 22
anglerfish 12
Arctic Ocean 4, 5
Atlantic Ocean 4, 5, 14, 28

B
Blackbeard 8

C
cave 10
clam 22, 31
clown fish 22
continental shelf 14
coral reef 22-23
crab 25
current, ocean 21

D
diving 28-29
dolphin 16, 18, 19

F
fish 12, 13, 16, 22, 24, 26, 27, 30
fishing 30

G
gills 16
Great Barrier Reef 23

I
Indian Ocean 4, 5

L
limpet 11

M
Magellan, Ferdinand 9
Mediterranean Sea 5
Mid-Atlantic Ridge 14

N
narwhal 19

O
oar fish 24

P
Pacific Ocean 4, 5, 29, 30, 31
parrot fish 22
penguin 17
pirate 8-9

R
Red Sea 7

S
sailfish 24
salt 6
sand 10
seahorse 17
sea mount 15
seashell 10, 11, 22, 25, 31
seaweed 10, 24, 30
shark 24, 26
squid 17
stonefish 27
submarine 28
submersible 28, 29

T
tide 10, 11, 21
torpedo ray 26
Trieste 29

V
volcano, underwater 14, 15

W
wave 10, 11, 20
whale 18, 19
wrecker 10